# 10 easy ways to earn money from Linkedin

Deepak Yadav

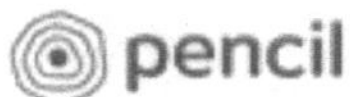

ISBN 978-93-5667-101-0
© Deepak Yadav 2022
Published in India 2022 by Pencil

*A brand of*
One Point Six Technologies Pvt. Ltd.
123, Building J2, Shram Seva Premises,
Wadala Truck Terminal, Wadala (E)
Mumbai 400037, Maharashtra, INDIA
**E** connect@thepencilapp.com
**W** www.thepencilapp.com

# CONTENTS

# Introduction

Do you want to get some information on how to earn money sitting at home or to advance your business?

So let us tell you that we have brought a solution to this problem of many people through this book.

Where earning money has become easy in the present times, it has also become necessary to take education of new technology because if you are not aware of new technologies then you are ignorant of many benefits.

From earning money by working part time sitting at home to taking business to every corner of the world through mobile and laptop, the power of new technology is hidden in the new technology, which if you know how to use it, then you can make your career very easily.

Linkedin is also one of those platforms which can provide you all the facilities sitting at home and gives an opportunity to earn money easily through its best features.

But before knowing about how to earn money, it is important for you to have complete information about the medium of earning money.

Unless you know how the medium you are working with works or what facilities it provides, you cannot know how to use it properly.

To use Linkedin, it is also necessary that you know what is Linkedin?

That's why first of all we will answer you this question so that you do not have to face any kind of problem going forward and you will also understand when we are telling you about which feature.

This book has been prepared in very easy language, so you will not have any problem here in understanding any subject.

Hopefully you will like the information that is going to be given to you next and you will find the answers to the questions you wanted here.

So let us now without any delay and interruption come to our main topic and know what is Linkedin and why people have started liking it so much-

What is Linkedin?

LinkedIn is a company of American Business Employment that works to connect us with people through online service.

It is operated through website and this platform was launched on 5th May 2003 which is mostly used for professional networks.

To give a right direction to your career and to get new opportunities, the use of Linkedin has increased a lot.

You can easily get in touch with big companies or clients by posting your resume here, which is its most beneficial advantage.

LinkedIn is a service that the Internet has provided us and it is said to be the world's largest professional network.

If you have LinkedIn in your smartphone but you still do not know what this application is used for or how it works here, then you are going to get all the information about it here.

LinkedIn is one such application that helps us to find the right jobs and internships through its wide network and it can be a great way to build a career.

Also you can easily use it on your desktop, laptop, mobile etc.

Under this application, you will get profiles of millions of people, which will include different categories of people.

You will find out further what works can be done here.

This social networking website is designed in such a way that you will get all the professional work and here you can easily share the information related to your business with the people.

Just like you get the option to create a profile on social media apps like Facebook, LinkedIn also gives you all the facilities to create an attractive profile.

It highlights your profile and presents it to the people in which your resume is there and only after seeing that people judge your work and not only this but through this platform you can also get in touch with your old and new friends. can stay.

LinkedIn has provided so many facilities to the users that today it has become famous all over the world.

All its features are very easy to use and here you will find people associated with almost all big companies so that you can easily contact them.

This platform has played a very important role in the field of career and business where you can also follow people like you do on Instagram and Facebook and stay updated with their new vacancies.

As we told you that here you can also contact with your old and new friends and relatives, which is possible through chat.

Here now you understand what LinkedIn is, but how it works or what we have to do to use it is yet to be known.

So first of all here you need to know that to use LinkedIn, first you have to log in to this platform, after which you will be able to know in detail about its features and all the features and earn money.

So let's first know how to register on the LinkedIn application.

How does Linkedin work and how to register on it?

To use any social media platform or application, it is necessary to register or login first, there is no need to explain this to anyone in today's world.

Today there is no such platform that can run without login, whatever application you download, you need to login first to use it.

Similarly, LinkedIn also asks to register before using.

The most important thing is that without registration, you cannot earn money using this platform, so before knowing about the ways to earn money from LinkedIn, it is very important to know how to login here and how to create an account. goes.

So let us now give you step by step information about how you can create your account on LinkedIn in a few minutes.

1. First of all you have to download the LinkedIn application from Play Store which will be done in few minutes.

2. If you do not want to download this application, then you can also visit its website directly, both of these methods are very easy.

3. When you will download this application or reach its website, you will first get the option to sign up or you may see the option of join in your screen, you just have to click on it.

4. After clicking on sign up, a page will open in front of you in which a form will appear, in this form you will be asked for some necessary information such as your first name, your last name, your email address etc. The task is to create a 6 to 8 digit password that is unique and you can remember easily.

5. When you have entered the password, you have to click on Join Now.

6. Now the next task that you will be asked to do is that you have to verify your mobile number and to verify the mobile number you have to give some more details here like you have to select your country name, after this You have to enter your mobile number here.

Keep in mind that you enter the same mobile number here that you want to link on your LinkedIn account.

7. After giving all this information, you have to click on send code and as soon as you click on send code, an OTP will come on your mobile number, which you have to fill in the given space.

8. After this your mobile number will be verified. Here you can also see the option to enter the postal code but it is optional so if you want to enter the postal code then you can enter and if you do not know the postal code then you can also skip this option and after that you Click on the Next option.

9. Now in the next step you have to fill some of your professional information, here you will be asked whether you are a student? So if you are a student then click on Yes.

After that you may be asked the name of the college or school, then enter the name of your college here, then you may be asked some questions related to your degree, if you have obtained a degree or the degree for which you are Enter the name of the one you are studying.

10. In the next option, you will have to tell about some of your strengths like what is special in you, then after this you can be asked in which year you started your studies and in which year your studies ended.

11. After this a box will appear in your screen where you have to click but keep in mind that you must be above 18 years of age.

12. After doing this, you have to click on the next option.

13. When you have done all these things, now a page will open in front of you where you have to select your category. Category means that the field in which you have interest like education or health or any other field then you have to select it.

14. After selecting the category, some permission will be taken from you, after reading which you can proceed by clicking on the bonfire.

Now the last thing you have to do is that you have to verify your email id, for which you have to click on Go to your Email inbox.

When you click on this option, you will be taken to your email id page from where you can successfully create your account on LinkedIn by verifying your email id.

This process may seem long to you, but when you follow it step by step, you will see that within a few minutes your registration has been completed and your account has been created on LinkedIn and now you can use it easily. can.

So now your profile is completely ready on the LinkedIn application, using which you can earn money.

But are the questions arising in your mind that there are many other applications like LinkedIn available on social media which provide such facilities, then why should LinkedIn be used? Or what are the benefits we are getting under this which are not seen in other applications?

So let us take a look at the benefits of LinkedIn to clear your doubts.

What are the benefits of using Linkedin?

As you mentioned earlier, LinkedIn is a professional working network that is spread across the globe and helps us to stay connected with our clients or employees.

This is a great social media website, under which we get to see many benefits.

Like have you ever thought before that it is possible to find a person from any company in any country?

If not then it is absolutely true because now you can contact any person in the world using Linkedin because on this platform you will get the profiles of CEOs, Managers and Employees etc. of big companies.

Linkedin is a very big stage which is being used by many people to take their profession to the right level, from where many people have also got a good job using this platform.

When you make a post on this platform and it gets a good response from the people, that is, people like, comment or share that post with others, then this post of yours reaches all the people associated with those people. Which is the best feature of this platform i.e. here your business reaches more and more people.

If you want to join a company from another country, then you can also do this work with the help of this platform and by following them, you can be aware of their daily updates.

The facilities you get on LinkedIn, you can easily reach people by uploading documents etc., but the condition is that its professional quality should be excellent, which people can give positive reaction.

Once you have contacted a company, you can easily deliver your resume to them or upload your CV to LinkedIn so that whenever someone visits your profile, your CV will be visible to them.

If you are a student and want to make a side income initially, then it is absolutely possible through LinkedIn.

We get many such benefits under this platform, so you can say that LinkedIn is the most advanced feature of professional network.

So you saw how you get more than one facility here.

Some such facilities are available to you on other social media apps as well, but the area of LinkedIn is spread as much as you will hardly see in other applications.

Now you are getting all the information related to LinkedIn application but which is our main topic that how to earn money from linkedin or what are the easy ways to earn money from linkedin? The information is going to be given to you further, so you are requested that if you want to earn money using this platform and want to know about new methods, then do not skip the further information given at all.

So let us now know what are the 10 ways to earn money from LinkedIn.

# Earn Money Through Client Acquisition

You must have heard about Client Acquisition before but did you ever think that it can also be a way to earn money?

If not, then here you are going to get all the information related to it, but first of all let us know what is Client Acquisition?

Because many people may not understand what this means, then let us tell you that Client Acquisition is a process in which you attract customers to your side, that is, to attract new customers for any of your business or those who are existing customers. Let's convert them to regular customers.

It is a process in which the customer or client is connected with his business at very low investment, in simple words it is a way to get more and more customers.

But now the question comes that how to earn money by doing client acquisition on LinkedIn?

So let us also give you this information-

As you have come to know earlier that Linkedin is a social media platform whose network is very large and it is mostly used for professional work, then it is also very easy to get customers from here.

If you do any business or are associated with digital marketing, then this means can be very beneficial for you to reach the customer.

If you do work like web design, then you need clients for this so that you can earn money by getting new projects, then using Linkedin you can easily find clients for your work.

For this, you do not need to work hard, you just have to put some posts here which define your work or you can also upload some photos of the work you have done before.

After this, if a client likes your posts, photos and videos, then he definitely contacts you.

In this way by finding clients, you can do a lot of digital marketing work like web designing and earn money.

The network of the Linkedin platform is so spread that even if you have 1000 followers on this platform, it is still a lot as compared to other social media platforms because 1000 followers on LinkedIn is equal to 10,000 followers of Instagram and also here when When a client likes your photos, videos or posts, it automatically reaches other people associated with them, so that your work reaches people from time to time and you start getting work automatically.

So if you want to earn money from LinkedIn through Client Acquisition then it can be very beneficial for you.

There are many such people who have skills but they are not able to get work, in such a situation, by creating a profile on LinkedIn and posting continuously, they can get the project by contacting people related to their work.

Also, the demand for these work has become very high today, so you can easily get a good salary every month.

In this way, Linkedin helps to earn money through Client Acquisition, which proves to be very beneficial for even small business, so if you also use this platform and get the project by connecting with new people then you You will be able to earn good money sitting at home.

# Earn money through Affiliate Marketing

You must have already got information about affiliate marketing through many websites or internet.

But if you do not know about Affiliate Marketing, then let us tell you that Affiliate Marketing is such a marketing strategy in which you earn commission by selling the products of others.

That is, here you do not have to make any product of your own, rather you have to promote the product, brand or company of others with the help of social media platform and in return you get commission.

Now it is clear that what is affiliate marketing but to know how to do affiliate marketing on LinkedIn, you have to understand this way of earning money from Linkedin in detail.

Under Affiliate Marketing, you are provided a link to a product or brand by a client or company, which you have to promote on social media platforms such as website, Instagram, Facebook, Twitter, YouTube etc.

So in LinkedIn you can find people who provide this kind of work to people and if you have a website in which frequent visitors keep coming and every day a lot of traffic is collected on your website then you can use it. You can take advantage through LinkedIn.

There are many types of clients present in LinkedIn, so you will not take time to find such people who want to promote their product or brand and want to increase the sales of their product.

So another way is that you can start affiliate marketing on LinkedIn itself because if you get millions and millions of people here, then there will be no shortage of people buying products or brands here.

When you start affiliate marketing in LinkedIn, you get more benefits and you can earn more and more money.

The network area of Linkedin is so spread that very soon people get a good response on any post, then if you upload a link related to people's product here and people visit and click on it. If you buy their products, then you get commission from the owner of that product.

The more people who buy the company's product with the help of the link provided by you, the more you will be able to earn, so there is no limit to earning from affiliate marketing, the more the product is sold, the more you will get commission.

So in this way affiliate marketing can also be done through Linkedin.

You can easily become an affiliate marketer by posting about the product you want to sell and sharing its link.

If we tell the money received from affiliate marketing in average, then you can easily earn up to 10 thousand every month through LinkedIn and it also depends on which category of products you are selling like That you get more commission on the products of the fashion category, you get a little less commission on the common product.

So if you can find people on LinkedIn who provide affiliate marketing links to increase the sales of their products, then you can easily earn a lot of money by taking some time sitting at home.

# Earn money by blogging on LinkedIn

Blog is such a marketing strategy which is running in high demand today or you can say that blog is the best way of digital marketing from which you can earn money.

If you are hearing the name of the blog for the first time, then let us tell you what is a blog?

Blog means to write information related to a topic, such as suppose you have a lot of information about online learning, then you write and post things related to it, that is, make people aware of it, this is called blog.

But how can I earn money by writing a blog through LinkedIn?

This question must have come in your mind, so let us tell you some things about it too-

People of all classes live in LinkedIn whether it is education or health, sports or marketers.

Everyone has a desire to earn profit by promoting their work and blog is the best way to reach their work to the people, so these people look for such people who have all the information related to their work so that they By writing a blog about your work, you can present it in front of people and earn profit.

So if you know how to write a blog and you can present a good image of people's company, brand or product through the block, then you can earn a lot of money by writing a blog.

On LinkedIn, you can find these clients who get blogging done and can promote their work on one of your websites or you can write and post a blog on LinkedIn itself.

Apart from this, one way to earn money is that you can use LinkedIn to drive traffic to your blog or website.

We run our ads on a blog or website, so if you collect clients through LinkedIn and bring them to your blog or website, then you can earn a lot from it.

Apart from this, if you want, you can open a DM agency on LinkedIn.

DM Agency means Direct Message Agency from where you can tell people about your service by direct messaging and earn money by writing blogs for them.

LinkedIn is a very trustworthy platform where you get to meet your real customers, so by doing this work for them, you will not have to face any kind of loss.

Not only will your website grow, you can also earn money through blogging by connecting with new people and getting projects from them.

Like we told that you can talk to people through chat on LinkedIn, then you will be able to easily achieve the project of writing a blog by sharing your experience with people.

So in this way money can be earned from LinkedIn through blog as well.

Here you have learned about two methods, the first is to block posts on LinkedIn itself and the second is to attract users from LinkedIn and bring them to your blog or website and earn money from there.

Both these methods are used a lot to earn money and due to the large area of LinkedIn, you get customers of every category here, so blog can also become a great medium of your earning.

But still many ways to earn money from LinkedIn are yet to be told to you, so definitely read this book till the end because there are many easy ways that you can earn money using LinkedIn.

# Make money by selling products

There are many people in our country who want to run their own business and want to grow their business by becoming their own boss and working on their own accord.

But due to lack of knowledge of the right medium, they are unable to do so, so here we are going to tell you how you can earn money through LinkedIn by growing your business.

If you have your own business and you do the work of selling products, then LinkedIn can be a great way for you to earn money.

Let us know about it in a little detail-

Suppose you have your own business and you do the work of making and selling products, but the reach of your business is only in the area around you and you are getting very little profit, then you will definitely want that your business Spread to every corner of the world so that you can get more profit and you start getting orders to buy the product, then you will create profile on LinkedIn and post review about your product on it.

You will find many customers here, in which some people will definitely like your product and when you create your profile on LinkedIn and post a review related to your product and also post some photos and videos of it, then there are chances of getting the order. increase even more.

When you will post your product, you will see options like like and comment on it where you can easily know about the response your product is getting.

The most important thing about selling a product in any business is that the quality of your product should be good and when the quality of your product is good then you will not need to do any other work, you will start getting orders continuously and you can easily You will start earning money through this platform.

Keep in mind that when you post a review about your product, you have to provide all the information related to the product there, such as which category the product belongs to, how much is its price, how is its quality, you have made it in making it. Do not forget to mention what items have been used and their expiry date.

All these things have a huge impact on the sales of the product, so when your customer likes your review, then he will definitely want to try your product once and maybe this potential customer of yours will turn into a regular customer.

So in this way the Linkedin application also helps in selling the product, so that you can continuously increase the sale of your product and earn money.

Here you can also do this work to attract the client towards you, keep the price of your product low in the beginning and when your clients like your product and they start using them, then you can gradually increase the price of your product. price can be increased.

If your product quality is good and people are liking it, then even after increasing the price, there will be no effect in the sale of your product, in this way you can earn a lot of money by selling the product through LinkedIn.

# Make money by freelancing

In recent times the demand for freelancer has increased a lot and if you are also looking for a medium for freelancing then LinkedIn is a very good medium to do freelancing.

There are many people who often keep searching on the search engine where to start freelancing work or where we can get freelancing jobs, then let us tell you that you can easily find freelancing work in LinkedIn.

So let us now tell you how you can find freelancing work on LinkedIn?

Often you must have seen that freelancing jobs are posted on LinkedIn or other social media apps, but LinkedIn is a platform where you get real clients, so you can get freelancing work by contacting them by direct messaging.

On the same LinkedIn, you get an option of the search box where you can search for jobs by typing freelancing work.

Under this you can do many things like Freelance Writer, Freelance Copywriting, Freelance Editor, Freelance Translator etc.

Freelancing means working independently i.e. when you work for a client, you get paid for your work immediately and you can work for many people at the same time.

Meaning you do not work for anyone but earn money by working independently.

When you search about freelance work on the search box, you will get many results from where you can select any post related to your work and apply on it.

The thing to keep in mind here is that when you search for freelancing work on the search box, then you should check the posting date of whatever posts you will show because there are many posts that are months or years old, so you should take care. That you have to apply on the latest post.

As in freelancing work you can do a lot of work in which there are lot of work like web developer, web designer which you will do sitting at home and deliver to your client and then get money in return.

It can be a bit difficult to choose a right option among so many posts but when you find your right freelance job then you can apply for it immediately.

There are many posts in which there are some conditions which you have to read thoroughly, if you can work by considering all those conditions then you can apply for the related post.

When you apply for freelance work, the clients posting for that work will see your profile and because they will give you work only after viewing the complete profile, your profile should be attractive.

In this way, by finding freelancing work on LinkedIn, you can easily find a good job and what work you want to do under freelancing depends entirely on you.

Apply for the work you can do well and take some time sitting at home and work independently and earn a lot of money in return.

In this way LinkedIn helps you to earn money by freelancing, the doubts that many people had about freelancing would have been cleared.

Hopefully now you can easily earn money by doing freelance work under LinkedIn.

# Earn money by becoming a Graphic Designer

Hearing the name of graphic design, the first question that arises is what is graphic design or how is it done?

Graphic design is an art in which you make a structure attractive and give shape to its texture with the help of color words and images etc.

For example, suppose you are doing graphic design for a website, then here you have to outline how it will look with the help of colors, images etc., simply put, you decide how a website will be designed and What will that view be and whatever things or features are present under it, in which place will people be able to see and how they can be used.

Graphic design is a very important component of the website which works to attract people towards it.

As long as your website will not attract people, visitors will not come to it, so the demand for graphic designer has also increased a lot in this world of website.

Nowadays every person uses a website to promote his work, even if he does not launch his own website, which requires a graphic designer because many people do not know graphic designing and people do not have that much time. Would have been that he could do graphic designing work.

So in such a situation, if you know graphic designing and you are looking for a medium from where you can get work to do graphic design, then you will hardly find a better platform than LinkedIn.

As wide as the network area under LinkedIn, you will find millions of people who run websites and are looking for graphic designers for them.

In LinkedIn, when you promote your graphic design work by creating your profile, that is, making posts related to it, then it may be that comments from people who want to get graphic design done on your post, then you can easily contact these people. can.

Apart from this, if you want, you can search by typing graphic design work keywords on the search box and select any of the latest posts from the results that will show in front of you and talk to its owner.

Direct messaging is a great way to promote your work because it increases your chances of getting work because if people need you then they will definitely give you work.

To present your work in front of people, if you want, you can share your previous experience with people, such as if you have done work like graphic designing for a website before, then you can post its photos and its reviews. Huh.

If your graphic design is attractive and people like it, then you will definitely find clients associated with it who would like to get you graphic design work.

If we talk about earning from graphic design, then as we told you there is no limit to earning in this kind of work.

You can do graphic designing work for many people at once and earn a lot of money.

The same graphic design also affects your earnings, that is, the more attractive your design, the more money you will get.

It totally depends on you whether you want to work with one client simultaneously or want to earn money by working with many people so there is no earning limit here.

So in this way, you can earn a lot by finding clients for graphic designing on LinkedIn and posting posts related to graphic design.

# Make money by editing photos

In today's era, who is not fond of photographing or taking photographs, but many times it happens that the photo is not clear or does not come well, then there are many people who look for people to do photo editing, according to them. Can edit photos.

Similarly, there are people running many YouTube channels who need a lot of photos for their videos, but for this they have to edit the photos and they waste a lot of time in this work, so they need to get this work done. For that they take the help of photo editor.

So if in the increasing demand of photo editor, you start the work of photo editor or have been doing it already, then you have chosen a very good profession.

If you know the work of photo editing well, then earning money will become even easier for you.

But now the question is how does LinkedIn help in earning money here?

So first of all, you have to understand that the reach of LinkedIn is very high, so whatever post you do here will easily reach the people.

But how to earn money from LinkedIn by editing photos, let's know about it-

The work of photo editing is a very professional work, which is needed by people every day, so you can either direct message and contact those people who have to edit photos or you can take a high quality photo taken and edited by yourself. You can upload your photo to LinkedIn.

Remember, when you upload your edited photo, do not forget to put a hashtag at the bottom of the post because when you post any content by putting a hashtag, then its reach to the people increases even more.

When people will reach your post and if they like it, then people will definitely contact you to edit your photo.

Here you can tell the charges of photo editing as per your wish and earn a lot of money and if you have already started the work of photo editing on any website and you want to promote it then LinkedIn is beneficial for you.

Here you can post the link of your website, on which visitors will reach your website and all the photos edited by you will be shown to them.

Even if people from there like your work, you will start getting clients.

In this way, money can also be earned by editing photos from LinkedIn, while if you want, you can also sell the photos edited by you directly.

If your photo is of high quality and is attractive and someone likes it, then you will not have any shortage of customers to buy them.

All you have to do is choose a subject for your photo that attracts people towards you like photos of nature.

Many people like nature and things related to nature, so if you have edited and posted a good and attractive photo of nature and you want to sell it, then tell about it, you can post it on your account and if that If you want to buy the photo, you can easily sell it.

In this way a lot of money can be earned by doing photo editing and photo selling.

# Earn money by selling your service

In today's digital age, the competition to get online service is increasing continuously, everyone is getting so busy that no one has enough time to leave their work for any service and search for people personally. People come to big platforms like LinkedIn and search for the service they want.

From here you can understand that money can also be earned by selling your service online.

On LinkedIn, you can easily sell your service and generate money in return for it, but as you know that any work takes some time to move forward and it takes some time to connect people to any service and trust it. It also takes time, so it is necessary that in the beginning you should take your service to the people in a small way.

What it means to say here is that in the beginning you can reach your service to people for free, such as writing content, writing e-books, editing videos etc. You can do the work for free in the beginning and as soon as people like your work. Looks like you can charge money for your service.

Under Linkedin, you will find many such groups where you can join and promote your service among people, but due to many groups, it becomes difficult to choose the right group, so you need to be a little careful.

On Linkedin, you can choose a group in which many people are already connected, where you can present your service to the people by posting continuously and after joining the LinkedIn group, the chances of your service being sold increase. go.

Also, in view of the increasing demand of people today, you can make changes in your service, as nowadays people like to read e-book very much because it can be read anywhere and anytime whether it is online or offline. So, if you make the service of e-book available to the people, then your chances of getting benefit from it increase.

If you want, you can also upload your contact number here so that you start getting people's contacts to get online service.

The more people find your service unique, the more the demand for your service will increase, so you have to keep in mind that whatever service you provide to the people, should be beneficial and unique in every way for the people.

Along with this, keep in mind that keep a good identity with the people with whom you live in contact, because gradually your service will reach other people through these people, then the better relationship you keep with your customer, the more your Service will be beneficial and you will not have any problem in earning money by identifying with the right people.

If you are completely new in this work and you do not have much knowledge about promoting your service, then there is no need to panic.

You can easily sell your service by posting a review of your service on Linkedin and reaching people because it does not require any high-technology, you can sell online service even after knowing some basic information.

In this way, LinkedIn also becomes a means of earning money by selling its service, the more people like your service such as e-book, the more you will earn.

So if you are looking for a good medium to sell your service, then you will hardly find a better medium than LinkedIn.

Earn money by working in Linkedin:

In the age of this technology, even big companies keep on taking out job vacancies, for which they also resort to social media platforms like LinkedIn, Upwork, Freelancer etc. can reach you.

So on this platform, this type of vacancy mostly keeps coming out and since you have also known that CEOs and managers of big companies are also connected on this platform, which can be easily contacted, so if you use

LinkedIn If you want to use it properly, you can earn a lot of money by looking for a job here.

We have often seen many people who keep searching for jobs on Google search engine or other social media platforms but still they do not get the job, so through this book we want to tell those people that Linkedin is such a platform. Where you can easily earn money by finding the job of your choice.

The number of job seekers here is not less, people often keep posting on LinkedIn in search of jobs and there are many people who have got their favorite job, then if you also become one of these people If you want to earn money, then you can easily get job in big companies by posting your CV on LinkedIn because business leaders are very active on this platform so your resume does not take much time to reach them.

You can easily get in touch with these big companies by using Haystack at the bottom of your resume or post.

If these companies like your resume, then you can get a good job sitting at home, but for this it is very important that you bring your good image to the fore.

From your profile pic to description, everything should attract people, and to make the profile better, you write all the things related to your work properly in the bio and do not mention the amount of work experience you have. Forget

It is not necessary that you should only put things related to your work in your resume, you can tell people about the qualities you have and the work you have done because all these things attract people a lot. Is.

If you have done a course, then you can also post about it on LinkedIn because if someone has work related to your course, then he can contact you.

It is also not necessary that your work should start from a very big company, even if your work is being started by a small company or a client, then this can be a good opportunity for you, which will give you a lot of experience. At the same time, your skills will also emerge so that you can be ready for the new opportunity to come.

You can also search for jobs on the search box of linkedin, where you will find different types of job vacancies and you can apply for any job you want, but keep in mind, choose a job that suits you or You have worked for him before.

In this way, you can earn money by finding jobs from LinkedIn.

# Refer and earn money

You must have seen the option of Refer and Earn in many applications, but if you do not know about it or are hearing its name for the first time, then let us tell you that Refer and Earn means to earn money by sharing the referral link.

This work is also exactly like affiliate marketing, for this you do not need to work hard at all, you just have to have a little patience.

The difference between Affiliate Marketing and Refer and Earn is that where in Affiliate Marketing you have to promote the product by promoting its link to sell the product, you only have to share the link to do the Refer and Earn.

Let us know about it in a little detail-

To refer and earn from LinkedIn, you have to join some referral program under it, which will be shown when you type the keyword on the search box.

You can join any referral program where many people are involved because such programs are very trustworthy.

After that you have to remove the referral link provided by that program and share it on your account and when someone visits your account and clicks on that link then that visitor reaches the site of referral program and when If that visitor creates his account then you get commission i.e. when someone creates his account through the referral link provided by you, then you get commission which can range from Rs 50 to Rs 500.

In such methods, the question often comes to mind that why any application or program provides opportunities to earn money in this way?

So it is obvious that the owner of any application gets the benefit only when more and more people use his application, so refer and earn option is given in most of the applications so that people can reach the people by referring its link. And more and more people create their account on these applications and use it so that the owner of the application is benefited.

Linkedin is a very popular application where many people run referral programs because they know that it is very easy to reach people from here, so you can join these referral programs and earn money by sharing their referral links among people.

In this way, Refer and Earn is also a very good medium to earn money and gives you the opportunity that you can earn money sitting at home comfortably without much effort.

# Earn money by working in Linkedin

In the age of this technology, even big companies keep on taking out job vacancies, for which they also resort to social media platforms like LinkedIn, Upwork, Freelancer etc. can reach you.

So on this platform, this type of vacancy mostly keeps coming out and since you have also known that CEOs and managers of big companies are also connected on this platform, which can be easily contacted, so if you use LinkedIn If you want to use it properly, you can earn a lot of money by looking for a job here.

We have often seen many people who keep searching for jobs on Google search engine or other social media platforms but still they do not get the job, so through this book we want to tell those people that Linkedin is such a platform. Where you can easily earn money by finding the job of your choice.

The number of job seekers here is not less, people often keep posting on LinkedIn in search of jobs and there are many people who have got their favorite job, then if you also become one of these people If you want to earn money, then you can easily get job in big companies by posting your CV on LinkedIn because business leaders are very active on this platform so your resume does not take much time to reach them.

You can easily get in touch with these big companies by using Haystack at the bottom of your resume or post.

If these companies like your resume, then you can get a good job sitting at home, but for this it is very important that you bring your good image to the fore.

From your profile pic to description, everything should attract people, and to make the profile better, you write all the things related to your work properly in the bio and do not mention the amount of work experience you have. Forget

It is not necessary that you should only put things related to your work in your resume, you can tell people about the qualities you have and the work you have done because all these things attract people a lot. Is.

If you have done a course, then you can also post about it on LinkedIn because if someone has work related to your course, then he can contact you.

It is also not necessary that your work should start from a very big company, even if your work is being started by a small company or a client, then this can be a good opportunity for you, which will give you a lot of experience. At the same time, your skills will also emerge so that you can be ready for the new opportunity to come.

You can also search for jobs on the search box of linkedin, where you will find different types of job vacancies and you can apply for any job you want, but keep in mind, choose a job that suits you or You have worked for him before.

In this way, you can earn money by finding jobs from LinkedIn.

# Conclusion

Every person wants that his hard work can reach the people and they can get the benefit of it, but due to not knowing the right medium for this or due to lack of knowledge, our work often remains incomplete.

Therefore, through this book, we have given you the same information that how you can earn money through LinkedIn application and can reach your service to those people who need it.

By creating an attractive profile in Linkedin, you can easily get jobs in big companies by uploading your CV.

Not only this, if you want, through your skills and passion, you can make your own business successful in other countries as well.

Many people are not aware that social media is not just a means of entertainment, if you are using the internet only for entertainment today, then you are missing a huge opportunity to earn a name.

Very few people know how to move forward by using their skills in this technological world.

But there are many people who get confused after seeing countless applications that which medium is suitable to work.

So in today's digital age, in the ever-increasing new application, where it is difficult to understand through which application you will get better results, Linkedin can be the answer to your every question.

In order to grow consistently, it is very important for you to connect with a large network that you get through LinkedIn.

Here you know how LinkedIn connects you from city to city, state to state and country to country.

You can easily grow your business using LinkedIn.

Here you have been told 10 such ways using which you can easily earn money through online medium.

It depends on you to do part time or full time job sitting at home, so you can apply for a job that suits your condition.

There are many jobs for which there are flexible conditions, that is, you can work anytime you want, so if you apply for this kind of job, then you get even more benefits and in this way Linkedin will help people with its service. Influencing even more.

At the same time, there are different classes of people on this platform, so that you can stay in contact with the people of your area according to your interest.

If you use this medium then your chances of being successful increase because their features are very good.

In this way, Linkedin also becomes a way of earning online, which if you learn to use it and once you move towards your interested field then you will see many opportunities for success.

As the technology is developing, the competition has also increased a lot, so today you will get to see a lot of competition on every earning platform, so that by competing with your participants to reach your right customer, you will get your service. Have to reach the people.

The biggest advantage in the benefits of Linkedin is that when you promote your work on this platform, you can reach more and more customers and where they find your service unique, that is, your good work starts from there. It becomes

Here you know how LinkedIn has made all the work related to the profession easy and apart from reaching your customers, you can complete all your work on time by managing flexible time.

So this was the information about all the topics related to Linkedin and Linkedin.

Here we have tried our best to answer every question that arises about Linkedin and we hope that you will not have any doubts about Linkedin now.

If you have liked the information given about Linkedin and now you are thinking of earning money through this medium, then hurry up and present your merits in front of people by preparing your profile on this platform.

Hope you like all the information we have provided and inspire you to move forward.

To get such new information and to know about new ways to earn money, do not forget to read our other books and stay connected with us because we will keep bringing many such information for you.